Contents

Any words appearing in the text in bold, **like this**, are explained in the glossary. You can also look out for them in the Star words box at the bottom of each page.

Father, footballer, icon

Football is the world's most popular sport. One of the most famous players is David Beckham. He is the sporting hero of millions of people around the world. He plays for one of the greatest football teams of all time. He is also captain of his country's team, England. Football is only part of the David Beckham story, though. David is as famous off the pitch as he is on it.

STAR ★ FILES

David Beckham

Paul Harrison

www.raintreepublishers.co.uk

Visit our website to find out more information about **Raintree** books.

To order:

☎ Phone 44 (0) 1865 888113

▤ Send a fax to 44 (0) 1865 314091

▢ Visit the Raintree Bookshop at **www.raintreepublishers.co.uk** to browse our catalogue and order online.

Produced for Raintree by
White-Thomson Publishing Ltd
Bridgewater Business Centre
210 High Street, Lewes, BN7 2NH

First published in Great Britain by Raintree,
Halley Court, Jordan Hill, Oxford OX2 8EJ,
part of Harcourt Education.
Raintree is a registered trademark of
Harcourt Education Ltd.

Editorial: Catherine Clarke, Sarah Shannon and
Kate Buckingham
Design: Leishman Design and Michelle Lisseter
Picture Research: Catherine Clarke
Production: Chloe Bloom

Originated by Modern Age
Printed and bound in China by South China
Printing Company

ISBN 1 844 43297 1
09 08 07 06 05
10 9 8 7 6 5 4 3 2 1

**British Library Cataloguing in
Publication Data**
Harrison, Paul
David Beckham. – (Star Files)
796.3'34'092
A full catalogue record for this book is
available from the British Library.

Acknowledgements
The publishers would like to thank the following
for permission to reproduce photographs:
Allstar (Sportsphoto.co.uk) pp. **16** (b), **26** (b), **26**
(t), **27**; Corbis pp. **9** (Reuters/Ian Hodgson), **10**
(Christian Liewig/Tempsport), **15** (Reuters/Russell
Boyce), **16** (t) (Reuters), **17** (Reuters/Russell Boyce),
18 (b), **19** (Reuters/Marcus Borga), **20** (t) (Photo &
Co/Manuel Blondeau), **22** (t) (Morton Beebe), **23**
(Reuters/Darren Staples), **24** (Reuters/Ian Hodgson),
29 (Reuters), **30** (Reuters), **31** (t) (Reuters), **33**
(Reuters), **34** (l) (SYGMA/Pitchal Frederic), **34** (r)
(Reuters/Toshiyuki Aizawa), **40** (Reuters); Getty
Images p. **4** (Gareth Davies);iStockPhoto.com pp.
12 (Eric Limon), **37** (b) (Joe Gough), **38** (t) (John
Kerher); Retna Ltd p. **13** (t); Retna UK pp. **14**, **43**;
Rex Features pp. **5**, **6** (l), **6** (r), **7** (Peter S. Bennett),
8, **11**, **13** (b) (Mark Campbell), **18** (t)
(Tang/Williams), **20** (b) (Action Press), **21** (Action
Press), **25** (Andre Csillag), **28** (Robin Hume), **31** (b),
32, **36**, **37** (t) (Jim Duxbury), **38** (b) (Robin
Hume), **39** (Sipa Press), **41**, **42** (b), **42** (t). Cover
photograph reproduced with permission of Getty
Images (Gareth Davies).

Quote sources: p. **7** Bobby Charlton, *Beckham and
Ferguson* (Jason Tomas, Sutton Publishing Ltd,
2004); pp. **8**, **10**, **12**, **15** *My Side* (David Beckham
and Tom Watt, CollinsWillow, 2004); p. **17** http://
www.rediff.com/sports/ 2002/may/ 03beck.htm;
p. **19** www.wldcup.com/news/1999Jun/19990603_
141_beckhamtalks_.html; p. **21** Alan Green, BBC
Radio 5 Live; p. **22** www.spicenews.com/html/
wedding.html; p. **23** *My Side* (David Beckham and
Tom Watt, CollinsWillow, 2004); p. **25** http://
www.geocities.com/Colosseum/Dugout/4039/
quotes.html; p. **27** BBC Radio 5 Live; p. **29** http://
news.bbc.co.uk/sportacademy/hi/sa/ treatment_
room/features/newsid_2129000/2129623.stm;
p. **31** Marcelle d'Argy Smith, http://news.bbc.co.
uk/1/hi/uk/1962668.stm; p. **32** *Time Europe*; p. **36**
My Side (David Beckham and Tom Watt, Collins
Willow, 2004); p. **39** http://beckham-incredible.
tripod.com; p. **40** http://soccer365. com/
EUROPEAN_NEWS/Premiership/page_99_61300.
shtml; p. **43** www.contactmusic.com/new/xmlfeed.
nsf/mndwebpages/BECKHAM%20TO%20STAY%20
N%20SPAIN.

The publishers would like to thank Rosie Nixon,
Charly Rimsa, Sarah Williams, Marie Lorimer, and
Nicola Hodgson for their assistance in the
preparation of this book.

David and his wife are a well-known celebrity couple.

Find out later

Which manager first made David the England captain?

Who is David's favourite sportsman?

What does David like to spend his money on?

Family man

David is married to ex pop star Victoria Adams, formerly known as "Posh Spice". This famous couple are rarely out of the newspapers. People always seem to want to know all about them. David and Victoria have three children called Brooklyn, Romeo, and Cruz. David is very protective of his three boys. He accepts that he will always be news. He does not believe, however, that his children should be in the newspapers.

Wealth and fame

David seems to have it all. He is a fabulous footballer and father. He has worked as a fashion model and appeared in advertisements. He has also been the subject of many works of art. All of this **exposure** has made David very rich indeed. Is this the whole story, though? What is it really like to be David Beckham?

London boy

Manchester United

Manchester United was formed in 1878. In 1968 it was the first English club to win the European Cup. This was a competition for the best teams in Europe. One of the heroes of that Man Utd team was Bobby Charlton.

David was born and grew up in east London. From a young age it was obvious he had a talent for football. David worked really hard to improve his game. He spent many hours at the park practising with his dad. While he trained, David dreamed of playing for the world-famous Manchester United.

Early promise

As a boy, David played for a team called Ridgeway Rovers. His performances soon attracted the attention of the big, professional clubs from London. At 11 years old David was signed for the youth **academy** of the London team, Tottenham Hotspur.

David dreamed of playing for Manchester United.

David has always been a keen footballer.

Star words   academy   place where talented young people receive special training

David was thrilled, but he still wanted to play for the team he supported. On his first day at Tottenham, David wore his Manchester United kit!

Winner

During the summer breaks David went to a soccer school. It was run by the ex England and Manchester United star Bobby Charlton. One of the activities was a football skills competition. In 1986 David won his local competition easily and went through to the final. The final competition was at Manchester United's home ground, Old Trafford. It took place at half-time during the Manchester United vs Tottenham Hotspur game. David walked out on to the pitch where his heroes played and won the competition.

> He is a perfectionist.
> (Bobby Charlton)

Crowd pleaser

During the final of the skills competition it was announced that David was from London. The Manchester fans in the crowd booed him. David's skills amazed the whole crowd, though, and they all cheered his victory.

Old Trafford is a huge stadium.

perfectionist someone who likes things to be exactly right

Making the grade

★ ★ ★ ★ ★ ★ ★ ★ ★ ★

New generation

Many of the FA Youth cup-winning players would go on to be the new generation of United stars. The team included Paul Scholes, Ryan Giggs, brothers Gary and Phil Neville, Nicky Butt, and David, of course.

★ ★ ★ ★ ★ ★ ★ ★ ★ ★

Scouts from big clubs came to watch David play for his local team. One day a Manchester United scout came, too. The scout liked what he saw. He took David to Manchester United for a trial.

The boss

After the trial, the Manchester United manager, Alex Ferguson, rang the Beckham house. He said he was interested in signing David to the club. David was too young to sign straightaway. He had to wait until he was thirteen. On 2 May 1988, on David's 13th birthday, he signed for Manchester United.

> " What could have been more exciting than that day? (David on signing for Man Utd) "

Alex Ferguson recognized David's talent and signed him for Manchester United.

Star words   graduating moving on to the next level
reserve team second choice team

A new home

David did not move to Manchester until he had left school. Instead, he travelled up to Manchester during his school holidays. It was not until 8 July 1991 that David went to Manchester as a **trainee**. It was odd being away from his parents. A new home and a new band of teammates took a while to get used to.

Winners

The team David joined was special. It was packed with hard working and very talented players. The team showed its class by winning the FA Youth Cup in 1992. This was the top cup competition for youth teams. The team would soon get broken up, though. Its star players were **graduating** to the first and **reserve teams**.

Paul Scholes was also a part of the young Man Utd team.

★ Star fact

Before he signed for Manchester United, David was the team mascot when they played the London team West Ham United.

vodafone

scouts   people who look for talented players
trainee   someone learning a profession, such as football

Alex Ferguson

Alex Ferguson is one of the most successful managers in the game. He has won over twenty trophies as a manager. In 1999 he was **knighted** for his services to football. He is now called Sir Alex Ferguson.

Off the bench

David made his first-team debut for Manchester United in a match at Brighton on 23 September 1992. It was a big day for David, but he did not become a regular first-team player. He was small for his age. Some people thought he was too small. By the 1994–1995 season David was still not a regular first-team player. Alex Ferguson called David into his office. David was afraid that Ferguson was letting him go.

On loan then back home

Luckily, it was not bad news. Ferguson had decided to loan David to a third division team called Preston North End. Football games at this lower level can be a bit rough. The games are more physical than in the top, Premiership league. Ferguson thought playing for Preston would help to toughen David up. It worked.

> " That month at Preston was one of the most exciting times in my whole career. "

A bad start

The next season proved to be an important one. Ferguson had sold some of the older Manchester United players. In their place came the youth team stars.

Eric Cantona was one of the more experienced players in Ferguson's team when Man Utd won the Premiership in 1996.

Star words knighted important honour from the queen

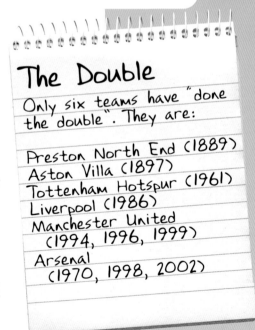

Arsenal "did the double" in 1998.

The season did not start well. The team lost their first game 3–0 to Aston Villa. The fans were worried that the young players were not good enough.

The double

The young players turned out to be more than good enough. Manchester United won the league, and in May they also won the FA Cup. This is the oldest cup competition in the world. Each year 500 English teams try to win it. Winning the league and the FA Cup, or "doing the double", is a fantastic achievement.

The Double

Only six teams have "done the double". They are:

Preston North End (1889)
Aston Villa (1897)
Tottenham Hotspur (1961)
Liverpool (1986)
Manchester United
  (1994, 1996, 1999)
Arsenal
  (1970, 1998, 2002)

A new hero

Wonder goal

David received the ball in his own half near the halfway line. He saw that the Wimbledon goalkeeper was badly positioned. David struck the ball high and hard. The ball dipped over the goalkeeper and into the net.

★ ★ ★ ★ ★ ★ ★ ★ ★ ★

Playing for England is an important part of David's football achievements.

David really came to the nation's attention during the 1996–1997 season. People were already raving about Manchester United's young stars. The young players were nicknamed "Fergie's **Fledglings**". One of them was about to fly higher than the rest. It all began at the start of the season. David scored one of the most brilliant goals of his career. On 17 August 1996 he scored a goal against Wimbledon from the halfway line (around 45 metres or 50 yards away). It was the goal of the season.

For England

The goal really made people sit up and take notice of David's talent. One of those people was the England manager, Glenn Hoddle. He picked David to play for England against Moldova on 1 September. David helped England to a 3–0 victory. From that moment on he became a regular England player.

Sharing his thoughts

Off the pitch, David's life was also about to change. In November 1996 David was watching television with his teammate Gary Neville. A Spice Girls video came on. It was their latest hit "Say You'll Be There".

She's so beautiful. I just love everything about that girl, Gaz. You know, I've got to meet her.

Star words   feisty full of spirit and self-confidence

Spice Girls

The Spice Girls (left) are still the biggest selling girl group of all time. They were formed in 1993 and had their first hit record in 1996. They had hits, including "Wannabe" and "2 Become 1", all around the world.

Spice of life

The Spice Girls were the biggest girl band in the world at the time. They were five **feisty** young women nicknamed Sporty, Scary, Baby, Ginger, and Posh Spice. David only had eyes for Posh Spice. He knew she was the girl for him.

Gary Neville is one of David's closest friends.

fledgling young and not very experienced

Nerves

David really wanted to meet Posh Spice. Her real name was Victoria Adams. Victoria was interested in meeting him, too. Victoria and Sporty Spice went to see Manchester United play. David and Victoria met after the game. David was so nervous he could not speak. All he managed to say was, "Hello, I'm David."

Low-key date

Eventually David and Victoria managed to arrange a date. They both wanted to keep their meeting a secret. On their first date they went to a Chinese restaurant for drinks. David and Victoria started dating and liked spending time together. The couple soon fell in love.

Mel C (or Sporty Spice) of the Spice Girls.

PFA Young Player Award

The PFA is the Professional Footballers Association. Each year, members of the PFA vote for the young player who they think has performed the best over the season.

David wins twice

Things were going well on the pitch, too. That season David played in most of Manchester United's games and scored eight times. These goals helped the team to win the Premiership. Fergie's **Fledglings** had done it again. David also won the PFA Young Player of the Year award.

⭐ Star fact

David and Victoria used to live near each other when they were younger. Somehow they had never bumped into each other.

Star words   importing bringing something into one country from another

It was not long before photos of David and Victoria started to appear in newspapers and magazines.

Will you marry me?

David and Victoria were both really busy with their work, but tried to see each other as often as possible. When they were apart they had long telephone conversations. David knew he wanted to marry Victoria. He proposed to her in a romantic hotel room. She said yes straightaway.

> It was like an electric charge running up my spine. (David on Victoria saying "yes".)

Love costs

David and Victoria bought engagement rings for each other. Victoria got a nasty surprise, though. She bought David's ring in the United States. When she came home she got a £3,000 tax bill for **importing** such a valuable ring into the UK.

A roller-coaster ride

The 1998 World Cup finals were held in France. David had played in all the qualifying games, but was not picked to start the first game of the World Cup. England won the game 2–0.

Same again

Managers tend not to change winning teams. For the second game, David was on the bench as a **substitute** again. This time an injury to another player meant David was brought on. He helped set up a goal for England, but the team still lost 2–1.

Hero...

The next game was against Colombia. England needed to win it. With the score at 1–0 to England David scored with a beautiful free kick. It was the first time he had scored for England. The team were through to the quarter-finals.

David's free kicks

David is well known for scoring from free kicks. He hits the ball very hard. He also twists his foot when he kicks it. This makes the ball swerve through the air. The swerve and speed make his shots hard to save.

David's free kick helped England to a victory over Colombia.

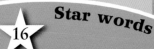

Star words

substitute player brought on when someone else is taken off, with an injury for example

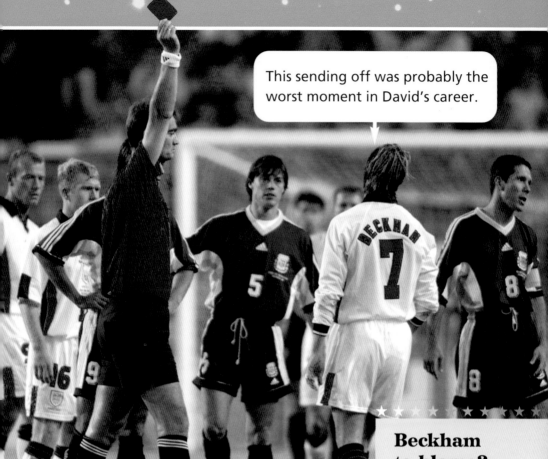

This sending off was probably the worst moment in David's career.

...to zero

England were drawn against Argentina. The score was 2–2 at half-time, but disaster struck in the second half. David was fouled by Diego Simeone. As David lay on the ground he kicked Simeone. It was a stupid thing to do. The referee had no choice – David was sent off. The team played well with ten men, but lost the game on penalties. England were out of the World Cup.

> "I went through every emotion. For a good 10 minutes, I just lost it."

Beckham to blame?

The day after the Argentina game, most UK newspapers were blaming David for the defeat. Many people thought that if David had not lost his temper, England might have stayed in the World Cup competition. David had a tough time ahead.

Getting away from it

David went straight from the World Cup in France to the United States. Victoria was on tour there with the Spice Girls. Unfortunately, it looked as if he was running away. Many newspapers wrote angry articles about him. They thought he should have come home to apologize.

Under pressure

When David returned to the UK, there was a huge crowd of **journalists** waiting for him. The police were needed to get David out of the airport. They advised him not to stay in his house alone. They thought he might be attacked.

Victoria proudly showed off her bump.

Ray of light

The night after the Argentina game was both one of the worst and best of David's life. He felt absolutely terrible about the game. Earlier that day though, Victoria had given him some fantastic news. She was pregnant.

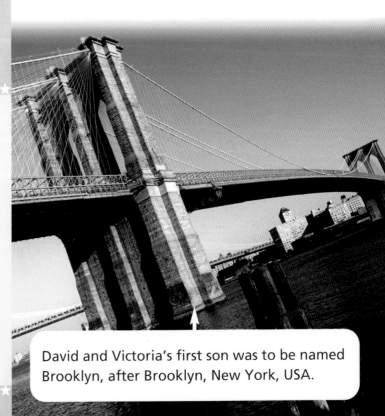

David and Victoria's first son was to be named Brooklyn, after Brooklyn, New York, USA.

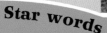

Star words   journalists people who write for newspapers or magazines

Many England fans blamed David for England being out of the World Cup.

Standing tall

Playing for Manchester United, David had always had abuse shouted at him by rival fans. Star players usually do. It is part of the game, and something they have to deal with. David did deal with it, and became a better player.

Top of the pile

David was in the best form of his career. It was not surprising that Manchester United went on to win the Premiership again. They also won the FA cup that year. They had "done the double" again. This year, however, they were on course to appear in another final – the Champions' League. Were Manchester United good enough to win a historic treble?

Staying strong

Many people would not have coped with the pressure that David was under, but somehow he stayed strong. He says, "If you go through an experience like that you can either crack up or come out and make people eat their words, which I feel I have done."

The Champions' League final

The 1999 Champions' League final was held on 26 May in Barcelona, Spain. United's opponents that night were Bayern Munich. Bayern were the German league champions.

The Champions' League final was held at the Nou Camp stadium in Barcelona.

Champions' League

In 1992 the Champions' League replaced the European Cup as the top European club competition. The highest placed teams in leagues across Europe compete for the Champions' League trophy. Teams that have won this competition include Real Madrid and Bayern Munich.

Centre of things

David usually played on the right wing. United had some players missing for this game, though, so Ferguson moved David into the centre of midfield. This was David's favourite position. He felt more involved in the game there.

David was playing in his favourite position on the night of the final.

Bad start

The game started badly for Manchester United. Bayern Munich's Mario Basler scored after only 6 minutes. The rest of the first half went by without any more goals. The second half followed a similar pattern. Bayern were in complete control.

Hanging on

Ferguson brought on two **substitutes** to try and change things. They were both strikers – Teddy Sheringham and Ole Gunnar Solskjaer. Near the end of the game, United got a corner. David took it as usual. He lofted the ball into the penalty area and Sheringham scored!

A memorable night

The game was now deep into stoppage time. David floated the ball into the penalty area again. It was headed towards the goal. Solskjaer was there and hooked the ball into the Bayern net for an amazing goal. The game finished soon afterwards with the score at 2–1 to Manchester United. They were European Champions. United had now also completed an unbelievable treble.

66 Manchester United rule Europe. I don't believe it, but it's happened. (Alan Green, Radio Presenter) 99

Winning the Champions' League meant that Man Utd had completed the treble!

Joy and strife

The Beckhams' Wedding Menu

Red Pepper Soup

Breast of Turkey
or
Grilled Mediterranean Vegetables

Sticky Toffee Pudding
or
Summer Berry Terrine

Off the pitch, 1999 was a big year for David, too. He got married, and his first child was born. David and Victoria wanted a fairy-tale wedding. Fairy-tales need castles. The couple were married in the grounds of Luttrellstown Castle in Ireland. The wedding ceremony itself was very private. Only 30 family members and the couple's closest friends were there.

Wedding party

If the wedding ceremony was small and private then the party afterwards was huge. There were nearly 300 people there. David and Victoria had a **marquee** in the castle grounds to hold all the people. After meeting all the guests, David and Victoria went to get changed. They reappeared wearing matching purple outfits.

> I've known Victoria was the woman for me from the first time I set eyes on her.

Luttrellstown Castle, Ireland.

Star words

marquee   large tent used for social events
privilege   something you are lucky to be able to do

No newspapers allowed

Journalists would have loved to be there, but none were allowed in. David and Victoria had signed a deal with a magazine. The magazine was the only one allowed to show photographs of the day. They paid the Beckhams £1 million for the **privilege**. Unfortunately, one guest gave some pictures to a newspaper. One way or another, the Beckhams always end up in the newspapers.

⭐ Star fact

David and Victoria's wedding gift list was very simple. They asked for vouchers for two department stores. Guests could make a donation to a charity instead if they wanted.

Another Beckham

On 4 March 1999, Victoria gave birth to a son. David was blown away by the experience. "I knew that, whatever else had happened or was going to happen in my life, I'd been blessed." They named their son Brooklyn.

Brooklyn is often seen in the crowd at his dad's football matches .

David and Victoria lived in Sawbridgeworth in Hertfordshire. This is over 320 kilometres (200 miles) away from Manchester United's training ground. Alex Ferguson did not approve of this. He thought David should live near Manchester. He also thought David was being distracted from his football. Ferguson did not like seeing photographs in the newspapers of David and Victoria going to flashy parties.

Worried father

One day, David missed training. The day before, Brooklyn had been ill. David and Victoria were very worried. David decided not to go up to Manchester for training that day. He wanted to look after his son. This did not please Ferguson.

It looked as though David's good relationship with Ferguson was in trouble.

Unhappy boss

David went to training as usual the next day. When Ferguson saw David he was very angry with him. He accused David of babysitting instead of training. They had a huge argument about it.

> Brooklyn is the best thing that's ever happened to me; being a dad is more important than football.

Frozen out

The next day David was left out of the team to play against Leeds. He was not even a **substitute**. Instead, he watched the game from the stands. This was the beginning of the end for David at Manchester United.

Celebrity dad

David is often voted as best celebrity dad in magazines. He tries to set a good example and thinks it is important to help out. He even changes nappies. David says, "I don't mind getting involved in the mucky side of things."

Kevin Keegan

Kevin Keegan (above) had a brilliant career as a player. He won **domestic** and European trophies with Liverpool. He was also twice voted European Footballer of the Year while playing for Hamburg. He has been less successful as a manager.

A truce

David and Alex Ferguson agreed to put the argument behind them. However, the relationship between the two men still felt strained. David was back in the team for the next game. Manchester United did not lose another game that season. They won the Premiership easily.

England regular

That summer David also played in an international tournament – the 2000 European Championship Finals. The England manager at the time was Kevin Keegan. Under Keegan's management David was a regular in the England team.

Down and out

England did not do well. They lost two of their three games. They were out of the Championship. There were other England games to look forward to, though. The qualification games for the 2002 World Cup were about to start.

Peter Taylor took over from Keegan as temporary England manager.

Star words

domestic   at home. A domestic competition is played in your own (home) country.

England lost the first game 1–0. It was a terrible match. No one played well. Keegan resigned soon after the game.

A great honour

Peter Taylor took temporary charge of the England team. They had a friendly game against Italy. Taylor chose David as captain. This is a great honour for any player, and it meant a lot to David.

Same again

England lost the game, but played well. David was **inspirational**. He seemed to be a natural captain. A little later, Sven Goran Eriksson was made England manager. He also picked David to captain the team.

David leading England out on to the pitch.

inspirational something amazing that encourages others to do well

Small bone, big news

The bone David broke was called the second metatarsal.
It is the long thin bone that connects to the second largest toe. Not many people had even heard of it before David broke his.

David played amazingly well in the Greece game – and ensured victory with his fantastic free kick.

Getting to the World Cup

England had qualified for the 2002 World Cup Finals in Japan. This was partly due to David's fantastic performances as England captain. Getting there had come down to the final qualifying game against Greece. England needed a draw to qualify, but they were losing the game. In the dying moments David scored a fantastic free kick. England had got the draw they needed.

Broken foot

England did have a worry before the World Cup Finals, though. David was injured. It happened during a Champions League game against Spanish team, Deportivo La Coruna. A Deportivo player fouled David. He broke a small bone in David's foot.

Star words   media types of communication such as television, radio, newspapers, and magazines

Huge concern

The **media** were in uproar. They wondered if David would be fit for the World Cup. Pictures of David's foot even appeared on the front page of some newspapers. People visited a waxworks museum in London to touch David's statue. They thought it might be good luck. Even the Prime Minister got involved. He interrupted an important meeting to say how concerned he was.

Broken dreams

Fortunately David's foot had healed enough to play in Japan. David was not quite match-fit, though. Sadly England were knocked out of the competition at the quarter-final stage. The heat and the lack of fitness stopped David from playing as well as he could. The dream of winning the cup was gone for another 4 years.

> Nothing is more important to England's World Cup preparations than the condition of Beckham's foot.
> (Tony Blair)

Three become four

There was some joy for Beckham in 2002. On 1 September Victoria gave birth to their second son. Brooklyn now had a little brother. David and Victoria decided to call him Romeo.

Even the Prime Minister Tony Blair was concerned about David's foot!

Fame

Part of David's appeal is the way he looks. For some people it is the main reason they like him. Magazines often vote him as being the most stylish man in the country. For many men, David is a style **icon**. They like to wear what David wears. They think it will make them look stylish, too. Even high-street shops copy the types of clothes he wears.

Frock horror

Not even David gets it right all of the time. He was once photographed wearing a **sarong** on a night out. People asked why he was wearing a skirt. The time he and Victoria wore matching leather outfits looked a bit silly, too.

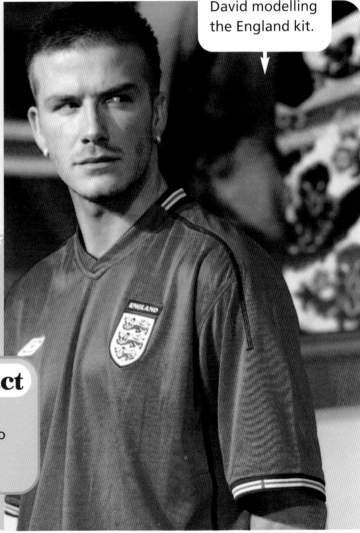

David modelling the England kit.

⭐ Star fact

One high-street chain hired David to design a range of children's clothes.

Star words   icon   someone who represents something and who lots of people admire

Looking good seems to come naturally to David.

Hair

David seems to change hairstyles as often as his clothes. He has had a **Mohican**, highlights, and cornrows (below). His hair has been long and short. Whenever he has a new style, hundreds of people copy it.

Fashion designers understand David's appeal. Sometimes they design clothes with him in mind. A famous Italian fashion label has called him their **muse**. David has also done some modelling. He always models the new England kit for the **media**.

Looking good

David had an interest in clothes from a very young age. Even as a boy he liked to look different. He has always taken care of his appearance, too. As a young teenager he made sure his hair looked just right. Now Victoria encourages him in his choice of clothes. She has a fine eye for fashion herself. Together they make a very glamorous couple.

> He's as daring with fashion as he is on a football field. (Marcelle d'Argy Smith, Fashion Expert)

muse someone who helps other people to have ideas
sarong long strip of cloth worn like a skirt

Star-studded evening

There were celebrities from sport, film, televsion, and music at David's charity dinner: film stars Ray Winstone and Sean Bean, TV chef Jamie Oliver, music stars Elton John and Goldie, and Gary Lineker and Sven Goran Eriksson (below) from the world of football.

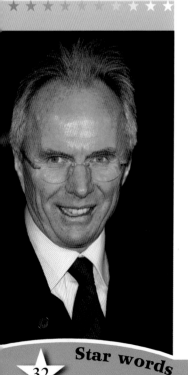

Doing good

David seems to have it all. He is a successful sportsman. He is also a famous celebrity. Lots of people look up to him. David knows the value of this fame. He does not waste it. Instead he uses his fame to help good causes. David does a lot to help those less **fortunate** than himself. He is particularly good with children. David often visits sick children in hospital. He has been to children's shelters, too. His visits really give the children a lift.

> " I like to talk to children. Sometimes they are ill or disadvantaged – it makes you realize how very lucky you are. "

Work abroad

David has worked closely with UNICEF. UNICEF is the United Nations Children's Fund. David and his Manchester teammates travelled to Thailand for UNICEF. They visited a centre that takes care of young girls. The centre got a lot of **publicity** when David visited.

Charity dinner

David's favourite charity is the NSPCC. This stands for National Society for the Prevention of Cruelty to Children. Before the 2002 World Cup David and Victoria hosted a **lavish** dinner. The dinner was held in the grounds of their house in Sawbridgeworth. It had been arranged to help the NSPCC. People paid money to attend the dinner. There was also an **auction** at the end of the evening. Over £250,000 was raised for the NSPCC.

Star words

auction when something is sold to whoever offers to pay the most money

★ ★ ★ ★ ★ ★ ★ ★ ★ ★ ★ ★

UNICEF

UNICEF was created in 1946. It was set up to help sick and starving children in Europe after the Second World War. Now UNICEF looks after children's rights to health and education across the world.

★ ★ ★ ★ ★ ★ ★ ★ ★ ★ ★ ★

David does a lot of charity work for children.

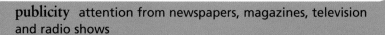

Fortune

★ ★ ★ ★ ★ ★ ★ ★ ★ ★ ★

Expensive tastes

David loves cars. He has had all sorts of different ones, and they are usually expensive. David has owned Ferraris, BMWs, an Aston Martin, Range Rovers, a TVR, a Mercedes, and a Porsche.

★ ★ ★ ★ ★ ★ ★ ★ ★ ★ ★

Fans go crazy for Beckham in Japan!

BECKHAM

23

⭐ **Star words**   associated linked with

Because he is a good-looking sports star, David has been asked to appear in lots of advertisements. David is popular with many different types of people. This means he can advertise all kinds of things. He has been **associated** with everything from soft drinks to razors.

Fans in Japan

Like many stars, David does advertising work in Japan. He has **endorsed** all sorts of things such as beauty products and second-hand cars! In Japan people also like to see him in advertisements with Victoria. They like the idea of celebrity couples as much as we do.

Big spender

David earns a lot of money from doing advertisements. He gets more money from doing them than he does from playing football. These earnings make David a very wealthy man. He enjoys spending this money, too. He particularly likes buying cars and jewellery.

Cheap wardrobe

David also wears a lot of designer clothes, but he does not spend as much on them as you might think. He gets given a lot of clothes. If David is seen wearing something, it is like free **publicity** for the designer.

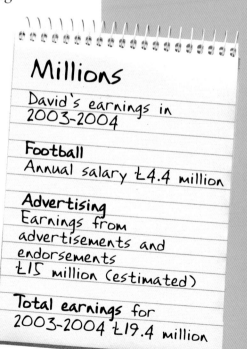

Millions

David's earnings in 2003-2004

Football
Annual salary £4.4 million

Advertising
Earnings from advertisements and endorsements
£15 million (estimated)

Total earnings for 2003-2004 £19.4 million

---

endorse when a famous person helps to advertise a product

Death threat

David has also had death threats. Once he was even sent two bullets through the post. It was probably just someone trying to scare him. David had also been threatened after the 1998 World Cup.

Sadly, fame can have a darker side and some people may try to take advantage of you. David discovered this in November 2002 when he found out about a plot to kidnap Victoria and his sons.

David had just finished playing in the first game of the 2002–2003 season. He was about to get changed when the manager called him into his office. Victoria was there with some police officers. They told him a kidnapping plot had been discovered.

> I was really upset. I felt my stomach turn over: it's anybody's worst kind of nightmare.

David and Victoria with their sons, Brooklyn and Romeo.

Star words evidence proof

The police outside "Beckingham Palace".

Fortress Beckham

Security has always been tight at David's home in Sawbridgeworth. The garden walls are over 2 metres (6 feet) high. The grounds have electronic gates and are covered by CCTV cameras. There are always security guards at their home.

★ ★ ★ ★ ★ ★ ★ ★ ★ ★ ★

The police arrested nine people, but a judge decided that the **evidence** was not strong enough to send any of them to prison.

An earlier attempt

This was the second attempt to kidnap Victoria and Brooklyn. In 1999 there had been a plan to kidnap them while they watched David play at Wembley. Luckily, the police had found out about it in time.

Guards

The second kidnap plot made David and Victoria change their security arrangements. They now have bulletproof cars. David and Victoria also have personal security guards. They have used them for years. After the kidnapping attempt they decided to increase the number of guards. Now they have six security people with them most of the time.

Time for a change

Flying boots can be dangerous!

During the 2002–2003 season David's relationship with Alex Ferguson got worse. If something went wrong, Ferguson always seemed to blame David. After one match, Ferguson was very annoyed with him. He kicked a football boot that was lying on the floor. It flew up and hit David in the head. It was an unlucky accident, but David still needed **steristrips** on the cut to his head.

★ ★ ★ ★ ★ ★ ★ ★ ☆ ★

Real Madrid

Real Madrid is possibly the most famous football club in the world. It is certainly one of the most successful. Real Madrid was formed in 1902. It has won more European Cup/ Champions League trophies than any other club.

★ ★ ★ ★ ★ ★ ★ ★ ★

The wound on David's head was very close to his eye.

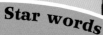
Star words   steristrips   stick on stitches used to seal a wound

On the move

Afterwards neither man really spoke to the other again properly. David did not enjoy the rest of the season, even though Manchester United won the league again. During that summer break David had some shocking news. Manchester United had agreed to sell him to the Spanish side Real Madrid. If David wanted to leave Manchester he could. The offer was too good to turn down. One of Fergie's **Fledglings** was about to fly the nest.

> I know that I will always regret it later in life if I had turned down the chance to play at another great club like Real Madrid.

David is happy to wear the same number as his hero – Michael Jordan.

New number

David had often thought of playing for Real Madrid, but it was very strange joining a new team. After all, he had been with United for 13 years. Also, David would have to get used to a different shirt number. Another player had David's favourite number 7. David chose 23 instead. This is the same number that basketball legend Michael Jordan wore. Jordan is David's favourite sportsman.

★ Star fact

David wears personalized football boots and has a new pair for every game he plays in.

Superstars

The team David joined at Real was fantastic. The Real team was nicknamed *Los galacticos* by the Spanish fans. In English this means that there are enough stars to form a galaxy. Being with so many world-famous players made David slightly nervous. His new teammates made him feel very welcome, though.

Los galacticos

The stars of the Spanish side included:

- Ronaldo (Brazilian striker)
- Roberto Carlos (Brazilian defender)
- Raul (Spanish striker)
- Luis Figo (Portuguese midfielder)
- Zinedine Zidane (French midfielder).

David had joined a team of stars.

Flying start

The new season started very well for David. He played in his favourite centre midfield position. He even scored some goals in those early games. David quickly became a popular player.

> If I have become a better player it's because these players around me have made me step up to another level.

Star words

civilian person who is not in the armed forces
OBE Officer of the Order of the British Empire

Honoured

There was more good news to come. In November 2003 David was at Buckingham Palace to see the Queen. He was there to be awarded an **OBE**. This is one of the highest honours a **civilian** can be awarded. David received his OBE for services to football.

All alone

Despite the great start to the season David felt a bit lonely. He was in a new country with a new team. His teammates were friendly, but David did not speak Spanish. For the first few months David did not even have a house. He was living in a hotel. Victoria and the boys were still in England. They had planned to fly out when he was settled. It took David a while to feel at home in Madrid.

Top seller

Real Madrid has made a lot of money from selling **replica** shirts with David's name and number on them. So far they have sold over a million of them. This is as many as the rest of the Real team put together.

The OBE is a great honour for a footballer.

Disappointing end

David spent much of the 2003–2004 season injured. He was not quite fully fit for the European Championships that summer either. England did not play particularly well. They were knocked out at the quarter-final stage.

Finally, David and Victoria had their own home in Madrid.

New hope

David was looking forward to the start of the new season, though. Jonathan Woodgate and David's England teammate Michael Owen joined Real that summer. David had also found a house. Now Victoria and the boys could join him in Spain. Victoria was pregnant again, too.

Happy home life

David feels very settled in Spain now. He and Victoria stay at home most of the time. They just enjoy relaxing at home playing with their sons. They can be themselves without anyone bothering them.

Michael Owen joined the Real team in 2004.

Star words   attitude way people act or think

Shaky start

Unfortunately the season did not start well. After a poor start the manager was sacked. When a permanent replacement was found, Real started to look good again. Things had picked up for Real and David.

> " I have a long term **commitment** to Real and to my life in Spain. "

Life after football

David is already thinking about what he will do when he retires as a player. The idea of managing a team does not appeal to him. He would like to put something back into the sport, though. That is why he is setting up a series of soccer schools.

New arrival

On 20 February 2005 Victoria gave birth to the couple's third child. It was another boy. David and Victoria called him Cruz, which is Spanish for "cross". Maybe one day he and his brothers will play football for England, like their dad.

David enjoys coaching kids and passing on some of his great talent.

commitment promise or agreement

Find out more

Books

Beckham and Ferguson: Divided They Stand,
  Jason Thomas (Sutton Publishing Ltd, 2004)
My Side, David Beckham and Tom Watt
  (Collins Willow, 2004)
My World, David Beckham and Dean Freeman
  (Hodder and Stoughton, 2001)
So You Think You Know David Beckham?,
  Clive Gifford (Hodder Children's Books, 2003)

Websites

David does not have an official website. These
two sites are worth looking at, though:
The official Manchester United site:
www.manutd.com
The official Real Madrid site:
www.realmadrid.com

Disclaimer
All the Internet addresses (URLs) given in this book were valid at the
time of going to press. However, due to the dynamic nature of the
Internet, some addresses may have changed, or sites may have ceased
to exist since publication. While the author and publishers regret any
inconvenience this may cause readers, no responsibility for any such
changes can be accepted by either the author or the publishers.

Career stats

David's career record (up to end of 2003–2004 season)

Club: Manchester United
Games played: 445
Goals scored: 86

Club: Preston North End
Games played: 4
Goals scored: 2

Club: Real Madrid
Games played: 46
Goals scored: 7

Games played for England: 44
Games played as England captain: 22
Goals scored: 10

Team honours

With Manchester United
FA Premier League Champions: 1995–1996, 1996–1997, 1998–1999, 1999–2000, 2000–2001, 2002–2003

FA Cup Winner: 1996, 1999

European Champions League Winner: 1999

With Real Madrid
Spanish Super Cup Winner: 2003

Personal honours
PFA Young Player of the Year: 1997
BBC Sports Personality of the Year: 2001
Awarded **OBE**: 2003

Glossary

academy place where talented young people receive special training

associated linked with

attitude way people act or think

auction when something is sold to whoever offers to pay the most money

civilian person who is not in the armed forces

commitment promise or agreement

domestic at home. A domestic competition is played in your own (home) country.

endorse when a famous person helps to advertise a product

evidence proof

exposure being in the public eye

feisty full of spirit and self-confidence

fledgling young and not very experienced

fortunate lucky

graduating moving on to the next level

icon someone who represents something and who lots of people admire

importing bringing something into one country from another

inspirational something amazing that encourages others to do well

journalists people who write for newspapers or magazines

knighted important honour from the queen

lavish rich and luxurious

marquee large tent used for social events

media types of communication such as television, radio, newspapers, and magazines

Mohican shaved head with a strip of hair down the middle

muse someone who helps other people to have ideas

OBE Officer of the Order of the British Empire

perfectionist someone who likes things to be exactly right

preparations getting ready for something

privilege something you are lucky to be able to do

publicity attention from newspapers, magazines, television and radio shows

replica copy

reserve team second choice team

sarong long strip of cloth worn like a skirt

scouts people who look for talented players

steristrips stick on stitches used to seal up a wound

substitute player brought on when someone else is taken off, with an injury for example

trainee someone learning a profession, such as football

Index

Titles in the *Star File* series include:

Johnny Depp
Jane Bingham

Hardback · 1 844 43283 1

Beyoncé Knowles
Mark Stewart

Hardback · 1 844 43296 3

Jackie Chan
Dan Fox

Hardback · 1 844 43295 5

Usher
Dan Whitcombe

Hardback · 1 844 43298 X

David Beckham
Paul Harrison

Hardback · 1 844 43297 1

Andre Benjamin
Brian Fitzgerald

Hardback · 1 844 43972 0

Mary-Kate and Ashley Olsen
Stephanie Fitzgerald

Hardback · 1 410 91662 6

Orlando Bloom
Kay Barnham

Hardback · 1 844 43284 X

Find out about other titles in this series on our website www.raintreepublishers.co.uk